D0282614

Thom Gunn

TO THE AIR

David R. Godine

David R. Godine Publisher
Boston, Massachusetts

Copyright © 1974 by Thom Gunn

LCC 73-89045
ISBN 0-87923-086-x

Acknowledgments are made to the *Listener, Iowa Review,*
Antaeus, and *New Departures,* where some of these poems
were first printed with certain differences.

Designed by Carol Shloss

Number 6 in the
FIRST GODINE POETRY
CHAPBOOK SERIES

Jan Schreiber, General Editor

To the Air

The Bed

The pulsing stops where time has been,
    The garden is snow-bound,
The branches weighed down and the paths filled in,
    Drifts quilt the ground.

We lie soft-caught, still now it's done,
    Loose-twined across the bed
Like wrestling statues; but it still goes on
    Inside my head.

Diagrams

Downtown, an office tower is going up.
And from the mesa of unfinished top
Big cranes jut, spectral points of stiffened net:
Angled top-heavy artifacts, and yet
Diagrams from the sky, as if its air
Could drop lines, snip them off, and leave them there.

On girders round them, Indians pad like cats,
With wrenches in their pockets and hard hats.

They wear their yellow boots like moccasins,
Balanced where air ends and where steel begins,
Sky men, and through the sole's flesh, chewed and pliant,
They feel the studded bone-edge of the giant.
It grunts and sways through its whole metal length.
And giving to the air is sign of strength.

Iron Landscapes
(and the Statue of Liberty)

No trellises, no vines
               a fire escape
Repeats a bare black Z from tier to tier.
Hard flower, tin scroll embellish this landscape.
Between iron columns I walk toward the pier.

And stand a long time at the end of it
Gazing at iron on the New Jersey side.
A girdered ferry-building opposite,
Displaying the name LACKAWANNA, seems to ride

The turbulent brown-grey waters that intervene:
Cool seething incompletion that I love.
The zigzags come and go, sheen tracking sheen;
And water wrestles with the air above.

But I'm at peace with the iron landscape too,
Hard because buildings must be hard to last
– Block, cylinder, cube, built with their angles true,
A dream of righteous permanence, from the past.

In Nixon's era, decades after the ferry,
The copper embodiment of the pieties
Seems hard, but hard like a revolutionary
With indignation, constant as she is.

From here you can glimpse her downstream, her far
        charm,
Liberty, tiny woman in the mist
– You cannot see the torch – raising her arm
Lorn, bold, as if saluting with her fist.

Barrow Street Pier, New York

Fever

Impatient all the foggy day for night
   You plunged into the bar eager to loot;
A self-defeating eagerness, though – you're light;
   You change direction and shift from foot to foot,
Too skittish to be capable of repose.
   Like an allegorical figure of pursuit
Which can't reach the end toward which it points its nose
   And remain itself, you're unable to engage.

Your mother thought you beautiful I suppose:
   Perhaps that's half your trouble at this age.
Oh how she dandled her pet and watched his sleep.
   Here no one watches the revolving stage
Where, joints and amyl in your pocket, you keep
   Getting less beautiful toward the evening's end.
Potential of love sours into malice now, deep
   Most against those who've done nothing to offend
Except not notice you, for only I
   Have watched you much – though not as covert friend
But picturing roles reversed, with you the spy.
   We seem to you a glittering audience
Tier above tier viewing without sympathy
   Your ragged defeat, your jovial pretense,
From brilliant faces that seem to smile in boast.
   Time to go home babe, though now you feel most tense:
These games have little content, so if you've lost
   It doesn't matter tomorrow. Sleep well. Heaven knows
Feverish people require more sleep than most,
   And need to learn all they can about repose.

9

The Corporal

Half of my youth I watched the soldiers
And saw mechanic clerk and cook
Subsumed beneath a uniform.
Grey black and khaki was their look
Whose tool and instrument was death.

I watched them wheel on white parade grounds.
How could the flesh have such control?
Ballets with symmetry of the flower
Outlined the aspect of a soul
Whose pure precision was of death.

I saw them radiate from the barracks
Into the town that it was in.
Girl-hungry loutish casanovas,
Their wool and webbing grated skin
For small forgettings as in death.

One I remember, a young corporal
I'd notice clumping to and fro
Piratical along my street,
When I was about fourteen or so
And my passion and concern was death.

Caught by the bulk's fine inward flicker,
The white-toothed smile he turned to all
Who would not have considered him
Unsoldierly as an animal,
Being the bright reverse of death?

Yet something fixed outlined the impulse.
His very health was dressed to kill.
He had the acrobat's love of self
– Balancing body was his skill
Against the uniform space of death.

THE GEYSERS

They are in Sonoma County, California. Till recently
you could camp there for a dollar a day, but they have
been closed for most of this year, 1973.

Thou hast thy walkes for health, as well as sport.

1

Sleep by the Hot Stream

Gentle as breathing
                      down to us it spills
From geysers heard but hidden in the hills.
Those starlit scalps are parched blond; where we lie,
The small flat patch of earth fed evenly
By warmth and wet, there's dark grass fine as hair.

This is our bedroom, where we learn the air,
Our sleeping bags laid out in the valley's crotch.
I lie an arm-length from the stream and watch
Arcs fading between stars. There
                          bright! faint! gone!
More meteors than I've ever set eyes on:
The flash-head vanishing as it is defined,
Its own end streaking like a wake behind.

I must have been asleep when morning came.
The v-sides of our shadowed valley frame
The tall hill fair with sunshine opposite.
Live-oaks are of it yet crest separate,
In heavy festooned arches. Now it's day
We get up naked as we intend to stay.

Gentle as breathing
                    Sleep by the hot stream, broken.
Bright, faint, and gone. What I am now has woken.

2

The Cool Stream

People are wading up the stream all day,
People are swimming, people are at play.

Two birds like one dart upstream toward the falls,
A keen brown thrust between the canyon walls.

Those walls are crammed with neighboring detail,
Small as an ocean rock-pool's, and no more frail:
Pigmy fern groves, a long web slung across
A perilous bush, an emerald fur of moss;
Wherever it is possible, some plant
Growing in crevices or up a slant.

Sun at meridian shines between the walls
And here below, the talking animals
Enter an unclaimed space, like plants and birds,
And fill it out without too many words
Treating of other places they have been.
I see a little snake alert in its skin
Striped head and neck from water, unmoving, reared:
Tongue-flicker, and a fly has disappeared.
What elegance! it does not watch itself.

Above, wet rounded limbs stretched on a shelf,
The rock glimpsed through blond drying wisps of hair.

A little beach and, barking at the air
Then pacing, pacing, a marooned brown dog.

And some are trying to straddle a floating log,
Some rest and pass a joint, some climb the fall:
Tan black and pink, firm shining bodies, all
Move with a special unconsidered grace.
For though we have invaded this glittering place
And broke the silences, yet we submit:
So wholly, that we are details of it.

3

The Geyser

Heat from the sky, and from the rubble of stones.

The higher the more close-picked are Earth's bones:
A climb through moonland, tortured pocked and grey.
Beside the steep path where I make my way
Small puffs of steam bloom out at intervals,
And hot deposit seeps from soggy holes
Scabbing to yellow or wet reddish brown.

I reach the top: the geyser on the crown
Which from the distance was a smart panache
Is merely a searing column of steam from ash.

A cinderfield that lacks all skin of soil,
It has no complication, no detail,
The force too simple and big to comprehend,
Like a beginning, also like an end.
No customs I have learned can make me wise
To deal with such. And I do recognize
– For what such recognition may be worth –
Fire at my center, burning since my birth
Under the pleasant flesh. Force calls to force.
Up here a man might shrivel in his source.

4

Discourse from the Deck

[MARGARET FULLER: I accept the universe.
THOMAS CARLYLE: She'd better!]

While Earth swings through the Perseids, curded blue,
The great landmasses rolling into view,
Through cloudflecks you can make out range and shore.
Stop here, above America at war.
Great varied land, of ebullience and despair,
Too green you'd think for guilt.
                                        And sink to air,
The gold hills, and a certain wooden deck
Outside a bath house falling into wreck,
Part shaded by wide figtrees, part in sun.
Fig-musk pervades the thought of everyone.

And here, a group of men loll naked, strewn
On planks that scorch in the long late afternoon,
In sulphurous dryness drinking whatever flows
– Jugs of wine, sixpacks, water from a hose.
I notice how, though on some they are mere traces,
Nipples are individual as faces.
But luck, embodied in such varying ways,
Like family happiness as Tolstoy says,
Causes the same look in far different people.
With flat or rosebud or tumescent nipple,
These strangers similarly talkative,
Generous, and joking, share the luck they live.

Fragile and rarely poised and vulnerable
Of course the place is. But in spite of all
– Even if predators and punks took over
Stomping or leeching those who have left cover,
Or if the dry hills and the buildings burned –
Nothing would modify the discipline learned:
To recognize, to accept, to understand.
To recognize I hold all of this land
Latent inside myself, including punks.
I'd better accept them – vicious, fools, or drunks –
Being carrier to their violence everywhere;
But hold it better from knowing it is there.

Such knowledge, like the figtree's smell, would then
Pervade the understanding and the man.
Ambiguous perfume! with which the air is full,
Heavy and thick and unavoidable.

Are these mere country follies, or could we not
Find other luck-inducers like this spot?
So many that they could at last be joined
And cancel the self-destructiveness of the land,
Until the America as seen down here
Would be the same as the land you see appear
As the globe turns, from high in outer space,
One great brave luminous green-gold meeting place.

18

5

The Bath House

Night
    heat
        the hot bath, barely endurable.
Closer than that rank sulphurous smell
a sharp-sweet drifting fume of dope.
Out of half-lucent roofing
                    moonrays slope
(by the plastic filtered green)
                      to candleflicker below.
Water brims at my chin
             breath coming slow

All round me faces bob   old men, pubescent girls
sweat rolls down foreheads from wet curls
bodies locked-soft in trance of heat   not saying much
eyes empty
         Other senses breaking down to touch
touch of skin   of hot water on the skin
I grasp my mind
          squeeze open
              touch within

And grope
       it is hazy suddenly
              I am strange
   laboring through uneasy change

whether toward ecstasy or panic
                              wish I knew
no longer know for certain who is who
Am I supposed to recognize
those bearded boys   or her, with dreaming eyes

  ..   ..

Not certain
            who I am or where
weight of a darker earlier air

the body heavily buoyant
                              sheathed by heat
hard, almost, with it
                              upward, from my feet
I feel rise in me a new kind of blood
The water round me thickens to hot mud
Sunk in it
            passive   plated   slow
stretching my coils on coils
                              And still I grow
and barely move in years I am so great

I exist I hardly can be said to wait

Till waking one night I look up to see
new gods are shining over me

What flung Orion's belt across the sky?
I lived the age of reptiles out
                    and I

  . .   . .

lighten, diminish
                    in the dream, halfdream
halfdream, reality
                    a flickering stream

beneath mud
          branching
                    branching streams run through
through me
          the mud breathes
                    breathes me too

and bobbing in the womb, all round me Mother
I am part of all   there is no other
I extend into
          her mind   her mountainous knees
red meadows   salty seas
birdbone and pulp, unnamed, unborn
                              I live

  . .   . .

                                        21

It tore
       what flash cut
               made me fugitive
caesarian lightning lopped me off separate

and born in flight from the world
                       but through it, into it
aware now (piercingly)
               of my translation
each sense raw-healed   in sudden limitation

I hurry, what I did I do not know
nor who pursues, nor why I go
I crawl along moon-dappled tunnels
                       climb
look back:
               they marked me all the time
shadows that lengthen over whitened fields below
calm, closing in
               Not all the plants that grow
thickets of freckled foxglove, rank hedgerow,
bowed bushes, laurel, woods of oak could hide me
But now
               I see a stream that bends beside me
quiet and deep
               and refuge I could stay within

reminding of somewhere I have been

hearing their tread
                    I dive in
                            sink beneath
wait hid in
            cool security
                        can't breathe
I burst for oxygen
shoot upward, then
rise
    to another surface
                    where I meet

 . .   . .

dreamers
            the faces bobbing round me on the heat
green moonlight, smell of dope
                            the shining arms
                                            and eyes
staring at me without surprise
I am trapped
            It will begin
pubescent girl and bearded boy close in

I give up
        hope   as they move in on me
loosened so quickly from it   I am free

I brace myself light strong and clear
think I know why I came back here
entering their purpose as they enter mine

I am part of all
                hands take
                                hands tear and twine

I yielded
        oh, the yield
                        what have I slept?
my blood is yours   the hands that take accept

 . .   . .

torn from the self
                in which I breathed and trod
I am

        I am raw meat

                I am a god